736/.98
More Hanukkah origami

P9-CAO-370

DATE DUE

Demco

More Hanukkah Origami

by Ruth Owen

PowerKiDS
press™

New York

Published in 2015 by
The Rosen Publishing Group, Inc.
29 East 21st Street, New York, NY 10010

Library of Congress Cataloging-in-Publication Data

Owen, Ruth.
More Hanukkah origami / by Ruth Owen.
p. cm. — (Holiday origami)
Includes index.
ISBN 978-1-4777-5715-4 (pbk.)
ISBN 978-1-4777-5716-1 (6-pack)
ISBN 978-1-4777-5714-7 (library binding)
1. Origami — Juvenile literature. 2. Hanukkah decorations — Juvenile literature.
I. Owen, Ruth, 1967-. II. Title.
TT870.O94 2015
736.982—d23

Copyright © 2015 by The Rosen Publishing Group, Inc.

All rights reserved. No part of this book may be reproduced in any form
without permission in writing from the publisher, except by a reviewer.

Produced for Rosen by Ruby Tuesday Books Ltd
Editor for Ruby Tuesday Books Ltd: Mark J. Sachner
US Editor: Sara Antill
Designer: Emma Randall

Photo Credits:
Cover, 1, 3, 5, 7, 8, 28 © Shutterstock.

Origami models © Ruby Tuesday Books Ltd.

Manufactured in the United States of America

CPSIA Compliance Information: Batch # CW15PK: For Further Information contact Rosen Publishing, New York, New York at 1-800-237-9932

Contents

Origami in Action

Hanukkah is a wonderful time for family and friends to celebrate with gifts, blessings, burning candles, and food. It's also a great time to get creative with **origami**.

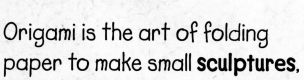

Origami is the art of folding paper to make small **sculptures**, or models. This popular art form gets its name from the Japanese words "ori," which means "folding," and "kami," which means "paper." People have been making origami models in Japan for hundreds of years.

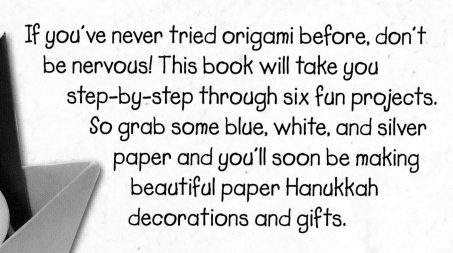

If you've never tried origami before, don't be nervous! This book will take you step-by-step through six fun projects. So grab some blue, white, and silver paper and you'll soon be making beautiful paper Hanukkah decorations and gifts.

4

Get Folding!

Before you get started on your Hanukkah origami models, here are some tips.

Tip 1
Read all the instructions carefully and look at the pictures. Make sure you understand what's required before you begin a fold. Don't rush; be patient. Work slowly and carefully.

Tip 2
Folding a piece of paper sounds easy, but it can be tricky to get neat, accurate folds. The more you practice, the easier it becomes.

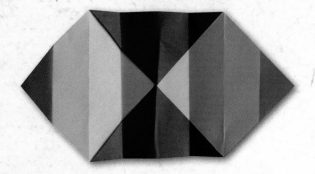

Tip 3
If an instruction says "crease," make the crease as flat as possible. The flatter the creases, the better the model. You can make a sharp crease by running a plastic ruler along the edge of the paper.

Tip 4
Sometimes, at first, your models may look a little crumpled. Don't give up! The more models you make, the better you will get at folding and creasing.

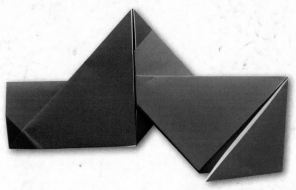

When it comes to origami, practice makes perfect!

In this book, you will find instructions for making stars and gift boxes. Just take a look at the complicated gift box and stars on this page. These models were made by experienced origami model makers. Keep practicing and you could become an origami master and soon be making difficult models like these!

When you turn the page, you'll find instructions for making paper Stars of David. You can turn your origami stars into a hanging decoration. All you need to do is use clothespins and a piece of string to create a decoration that's quick to make but has a cool vintage look!

Origami Star of David

The six-pointed Star of David has been used as a **symbol** on Jewish prayer books, religious objects, and buildings for more than 1,000 years. The star has also been an **emblem** of the Jewish people.

The Star of David is usually shown in blue and white. These colors are also associated with the Jewish people. Blue and white are the colors of the *tallit*, the prayer shawl worn over the shoulders at Jewish Sabbath, holiday, and morning services.

In this first project you will learn how to make origami six-pointed stars using blue and white paper.

A Star of David symbol on a Jewish synagogue, or temple

To make a Star of David, you will need:

One sheet of paper that's blue, white, or silver

(Origami paper is sometimes colored on both sides or white on one side.)

STEP 1:
Begin with a piece of paper that is rectangular.

STEP 2:
Place the paper colored-side down, fold in half, and crease.

Top left-hand point should touch the center crease.

STEP 3:
Unfold the crease you've just made. Now fold down the top left-hand corner so that the point touches the center crease and the bottom left-hand corner forms a sharp point. Crease well.

The bottom left-hand corner should form a point once the fold is made.

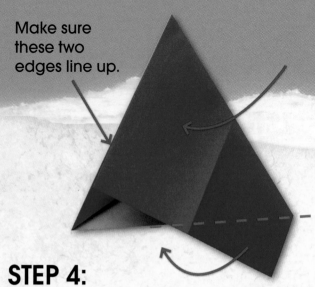

Make sure these two edges line up.

STEP 4:

Now fold down the top right-hand corner of the model so that it forms a triangle shape and the two edges of the paper line up on the left-hand side. Crease well.

Fold up the bottom right-hand point of the model along the dotted line, and tuck it inside the model.

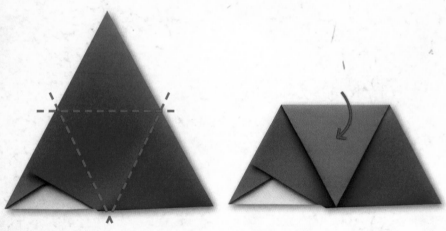

STEP 5:

Fold down the top point of the model so it meets the base of the model, crease hard, and unfold.

Now repeat on the two side points of the model.

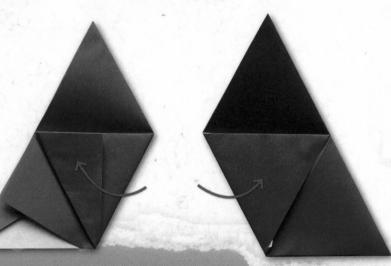

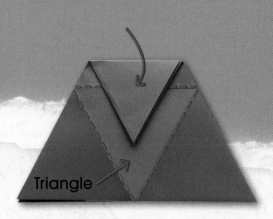

Triangle

STEP 6:

Turn the model over. Fold down the top point of the model so the point touches the middle of the triangle in the center of the model, crease hard, and unfold.

Now repeat on the two side points of the model. Your model should now have six creases and look like this.

Pleat

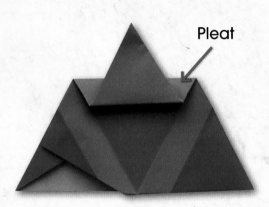

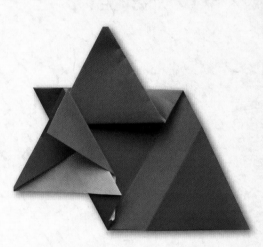

STEP 7:

Turn the model back over. Now using the creases you made in steps 5 and 6, create a pleat in the top point of the model. Then make a pleat with the left-hand point of the model.

Finally, make a pleat with the right-hand point of the model. Then tuck this pleat under one of the others to secure all three pleats.

Turn your star over, and it is complete!

Origami Hanukkah Wreath

Wreaths are a popular decoration during many holidays.

This Hanukkah, decorate your home with this fantastic wreath that's made completely from paper. You can use origami paper in white and shades of blue. You can also recycle gift-wrapping paper to add silver or patterned effects to your wreath.

The wreath is a modular model, which means it's made in small sections that are then slotted together. You can keep your wreath simple by just making the basic design, or decorate it with Hanukkah symbols such as the stars you made in the first project. Have fun!

To make a wreath, you will need:

8 sheets of paper in your choice of blue, white, or silver. Eight pieces of paper, each measuring 6 inches (15 cm) square, will make a wreath with a diameter of about 10 inches (25 cm).

Glue

Decorations for the wreath, such as paper Stars of David

(Origami paper is sometimes colored on both sides or white on one side.)

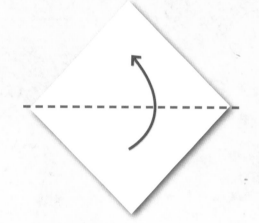

STEP 1:
Place the paper colored-side down, fold in half diagonally, and crease.

STEP 2:
Now fold up the right-hand point of the model, and crease hard.

STEP 3:
Then fold the top layer back down again along the dotted line, and crease hard.

13

STEP 4:
The right-hand point will have formed a small pocket. Gently open up the pocket and then carefully squash and flatten it back down so it forms a square.

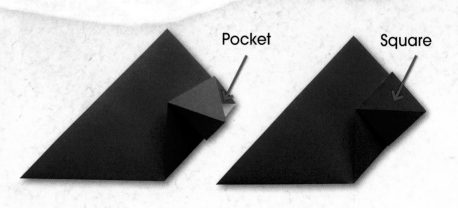

Pocket   Square

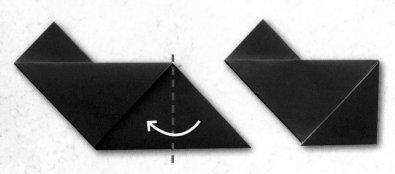

STEP 5:
Turn the model over. Fold down the top layer of paper along the dotted line, and crease.

STEP 6:
Fold in the right-hand point of the model, and crease hard.

STEP 7:
Turn the model back over, and your first module is complete. Repeat steps 1 to 6 with each of the other pieces of paper until you have eight modules in total.

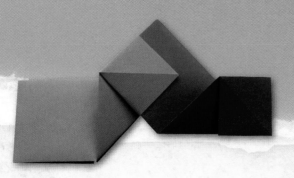

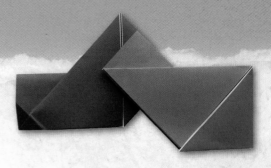

STEP 8:

Now take two modules and slot them together as shown.

Turn the model over and the two modules should look like this.

Now, folding along the dotted line, fold back the point of the light blue module so it tucks under and inside the part of the dark blue module directly beneath it.

Point

This fold will join the two modules, but for added security you can also tape or glue them together.

Keep joining the modules together, and finally attach module one to module eight to complete the wreath. Glue Stars of David or other decorations to your wreath.

Tealight Origami Menorah

Hanukkah is also known as the Festival of Lights. It celebrates a **miracle** that happened more than 2,000 years ago. At that time, the Jews were ruled by the Syrian-Greeks, who tried to force the Jews to give up their religion. The Jews fought back, and won. When they went to rededicate their temple by lighting the holy lamp, there was only enough oil for one day. The oil miraculously lasted for eight days, however, until more oil arrived.

During Hanukkah, Jews light candles every evening in a menorah. A menorah holds eight candles, one for each day of the miracle, and a ninth candle called the *shammash*, which is used to light the others. This year, using nine tealights and your paper folding skills, try making a simple origami menorah.

To make an origami tealight menorah, you will need:

18 squares of paper in your choice of white, silver, and shades of blue

9 tealight candles or 9 LED tealights

(Origami paper is sometimes colored on both sides or white on one side.)

STEP 1:

To make each candleholder, you will need two pieces of paper in different colors. Begin by placing one sheet of paper with the color you want facing up. We chose dark blue.

Fold the paper in half from side to side, crease, and unfold. Then fold up the bottom half of the paper, and crease.

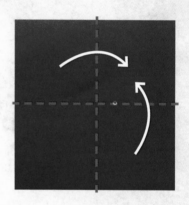

STEP 2:

Now fold the paper in half again, crease well, and then unfold.

STEP 3:

Now fold up the two bottom corners of the model so they meet the center crease, and crease hard.

STEP 4:

Now, folding only the top layer of paper, fold down the two top corners, and crease.

STEP 5:
Fold down the top flap of the model, and crease.

STEP 6:
Turn the model over, and it should look like this.

Now fold down the top two corners so they meet the center crease, and crease well.

STEP 7:
Fold down the top half of the model, and crease. Your model should now look like this.

STEP 8:
Fold the model in half, crease hard, and unfold. Then fold down the right-hand side of the model so it lines up with the center crease you've just made.

Next, fold down the left-hand side of the model.

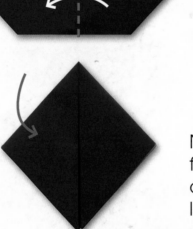

Now unfold the two folds you've just made, and your model should look like this.

STEP 9:
Finally, gently open out the model along the long, top edge so it forms a boat shape. The creases you made in Step 8 will allow you to flatten the base of the candleholder so it sits flat on a tabletop.

STEP 10:
Now make a second boat-shaped section and sit one inside the other. The candleholder is now complete.

STEP 11:
Make another eight candleholders, add your candles or LED tealights, and your lights are ready to be arranged to create a menorah.

SAFETY ADVICE
Never leave your lighted tealight candles unattended.

Hanukkah Treats Basket

This next project shows you how to make cute origami baskets for serving candy, fruit and nuts, cookies, and other Hanukkah treats. A square of origami paper that's 6 inches (15 cm) square will make a small basket that measures about 2 inches (5 cm) across. Just right for a small serving of candy.

To make a basket, you will need:

Two sheets of paper in your choice of blue, white, or silver

Glue

Scissors

(Origami paper is sometimes colored on both sides or white on one side.)

STEP 1:

We chose to make a basket that's pale blue with dark blue patterns, so we began by placing the paper with the pale blue facing up.

Fold in half from side to side, crease, and then unfold. Fold in half from top to bottom, crease, and unfold.

STEP 2:

Turn the paper over. Fold in half from side to side, crease, and then unfold. Fold in half from top to bottom, crease, and unfold.

STEP 3:

Your piece of paper should now look like this.

Using the creases you made in Steps 1 and 2, fold up the paper by bringing point A in to meet point B, and point C down to meet point D.

Collapse and flatten the model to form a square.

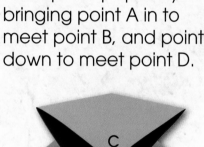

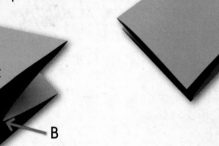

Open points

STEP 4:

Now turn the model 180 degrees so the open points are at the top. Then fold down the top layer of paper along the dotted line, and crease.

STEP 5:

Now fold the top layer of paper back up again so the bottom point meets the center of the model, and crease.

Then fold the top layer up one more time, and crease.

STEP 6:

Next, take hold of the right-hand point of the model, and working only with the top layer of paper, fold the right-hand side toward the left-hand side. Just like turning the page of a book.

Then fold the point back toward the right-hand side so it meets the center of the model, and crease.

Now fold the section of the model you've been working with back toward the right-hand side. Again, just like turning the page of a book.

Repeat everything in Step 6 on the left-hand side of the model.

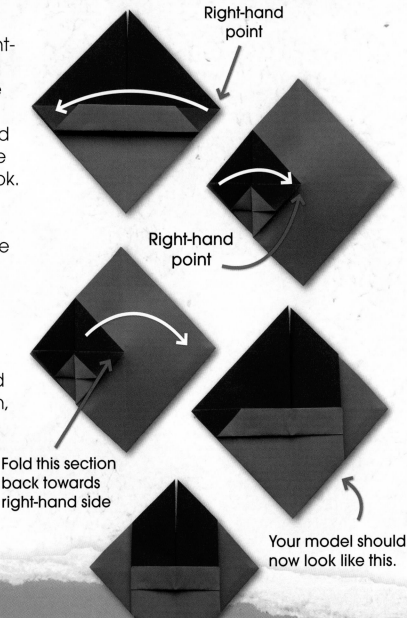

Right-hand point

Right-hand point

Fold this section back towards right-hand side

Your model should now look like this.

22

STEP 7:

Turn the model over and repeat steps 4 to 6. Your model should now look like this.

STEP 8:

Fold up the bottom of the model along the dotted line, crease hard, and unfold.

Now take hold of points A and B and gently pull them apart. The basket will start to pop open. Then you will carefully need to open out the base of the basket, flatten the bottom, and smooth out all the corners and edges.

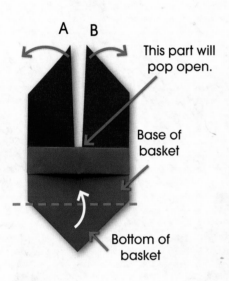

A B

This part will pop open.

Base of basket

Bottom of basket

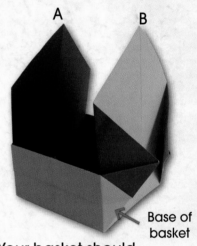

A B

Base of basket

Your basket should now look like this.

STEP 9:

Fold down points A and B along the dotted lines, and tuck them neatly inside the basket. If you wish you can glue them in place.

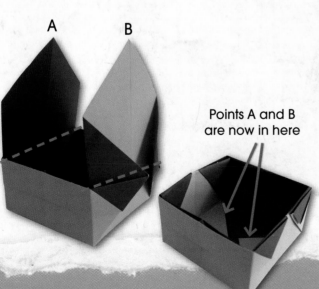

A B

Points A and B are now in here

STEP 10:

Finally, to make the basket's handle, cut a thick strip of paper from the second sheet. Fold it into three and glue the edge down.

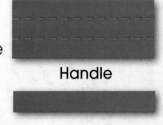

Handle

Slot the ends of the handle into the sides of the basket and glue them in place.

Origami Gift Box

Hanukkah is a time for giving gifts. So this year why not make pretty boxes for your gifts using your origami skills?

This next project shows you how to make a box with a lid. You can make miniboxes from squares of origami paper for small items such as jewelry or candy. Or make larger boxes from sheets of thick gift-wrapping paper. As long as you start with a square piece of paper, the design will work no matter the size of your paper.

Your friends and family will love receiving a Hanukkah gift in a handmade, **unique** gift box.

To make a box, you will need:

Two sheets of paper in your choice of colors
(one sheet should be slightly smaller then the other)

(Origami paper is sometimes colored on both sides or white on one side.)

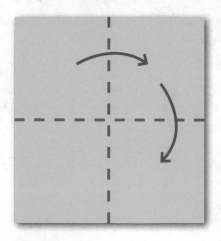

STEP 1:
Place the paper colored-side down. Fold in half from side to side, crease, and unfold. Fold in half from top to bottom, crease, and unfold.

STEP 2:
Now fold each of the four corners into the center of the model, and crease each edge well.

STEP 3:
Fold the top and the bottom of the model into the center, and crease hard.

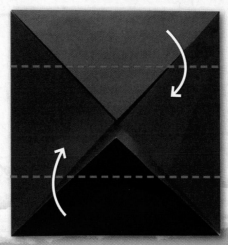

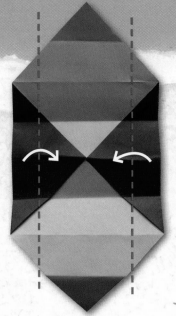

STEP 4:
Unfold the top and bottom points of the model and smooth them flat.

STEP 5:
Now fold the sides of the model into the center, and crease well.

STEP 6:
Fold the top of the model toward the left-hand along the dotted line, crease well, and unfold. Then repeat on the other side.

Then repeat this step on the bottom of the model.

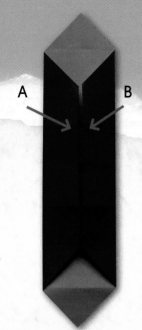

A B

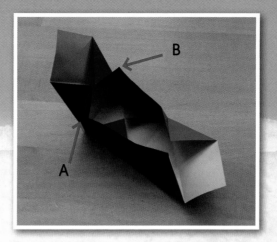

B

A

STEP 7:

Now take hold of points A and B and gently open them out. As you do this, the top of the model will rise up.

Fold the top point of the model inside the box and crease all the edges to shape the top edge of the box.

Repeat on the bottom of the model, and one half of your gift box is complete.

STEP 8:

Now take the second piece of paper and repeat all the steps to make the other half of the box.

Origami Gift Bow

In this final project, you will learn how to make a pretty paper bow that you can use to decorate a Hanukkah gift. You can make your bow from origami paper or recycled gift-wrapping paper.

You can even write a personal message in the center of your bow, to turn it into a bow and gift tag all in one. Have fun folding!

To make the origami bow, you will need:

Pen

One sheet of paper in your choice of color

(Origami paper is sometimes colored on both sides or white on one side.)

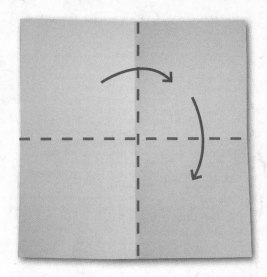

STEP 1:
Place the paper colored-side down. Fold in half from side to side, crease, and unfold. Fold in half from top to bottom, crease, and unfold.

Happy
Hanukkah

STEP 2:
In the center of the paper write a short Hanukkah message. The message can only fill about 1 square inch (2.5 sq cm) of paper.

STEP 3:
Now fold the four corners of the paper into the center and crease.

STEP 4:
Fold the four corners into the center of the model again, and crease well.

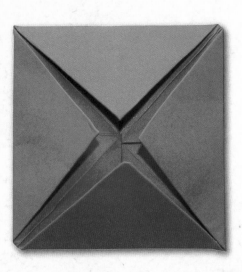

STEP 5:
Now fold the model's four corners into the center for a final time. The paper will be very thick, so crease hard.

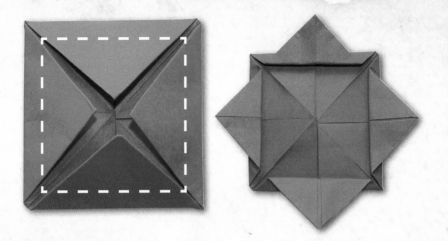

STEP 6:
Fold the four top flaps of the model back along the dotted lines, and crease well.

STEP 7:
Now fold the next four flaps that are inside the model back on themselves, and crease.

STEP 8:
Finally, fold the last four flaps in the center of the model back on themselves, and crease. Your message will now be revealed!

Happy Hanukkah

Glossary

emblem (EHM-blehm) A symbol used by a person or group of people as a means of identification.

miracle (MEER-uh-kul) An unexpected and favorable event that is not easily explained by science and that some may consider to be the work of a supreme being.

origami (or-uh-GAH-mee) The art of folding paper into decorative shapes or objects.

sculptures (SKULP-cherz) Works of art that have a shape to them, such as statues or carved objects, and may be made of wood, stone, metal, plaster, or even paper.

symbol (SIM-bul) Something that stands for or represents another thing, such as an important event or person. For example, a Star of David is a symbol of Judaism.

unique (yoo-NEEK) One of a kind.

Index

Websites

Due to the changing nature of Internet links, PowerKids Press has developed an online list of websites related to the subject of this book. This site is updated regularly. Please use this link to access the list:
www.powerkidslinks.com/ho/hanu